Nature's
RECORD-BREAKERS

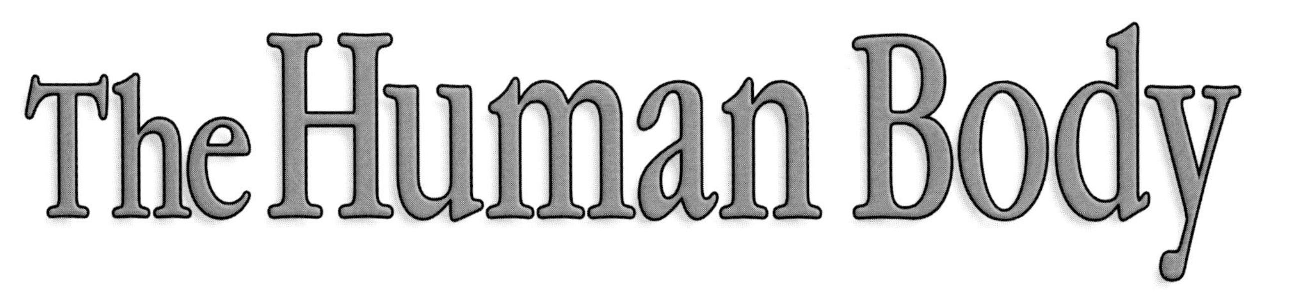
The Human Body

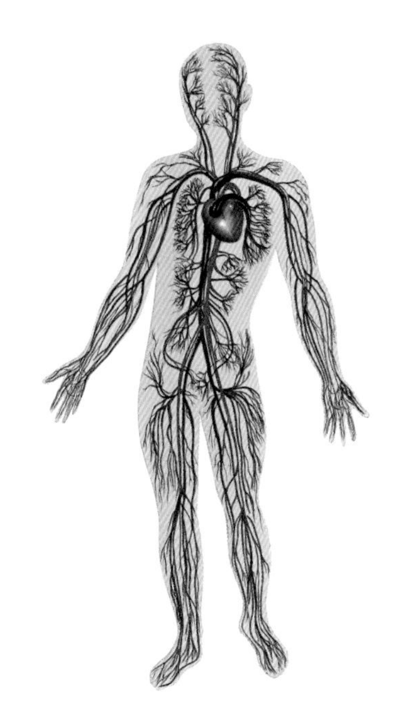

Written by Stephen Bruno

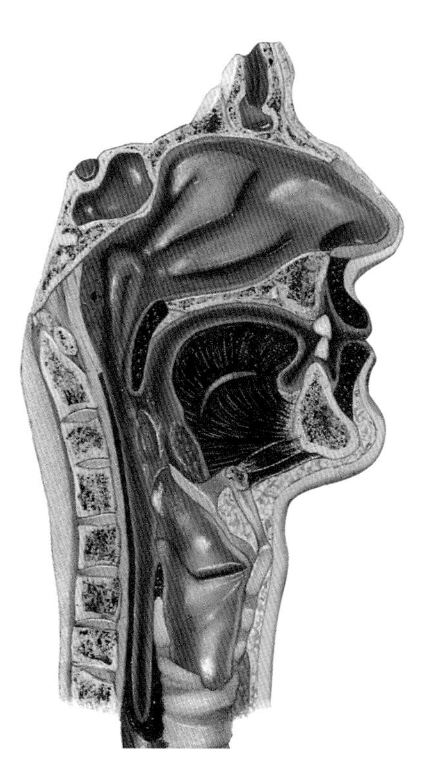

Illustrated by Alessandro Cantucci, Fabiano Fabbrucci, Sauro Giampaia,
Andrea Morandi, Gian Paolo Faleschini, Paola Holguín,
Antonella Pastorelli, Paola Ravaglia, and Ivan Stalio

Gareth Stevens Publishing
A WORLD ALMANAC EDUCATION GROUP COMPANY

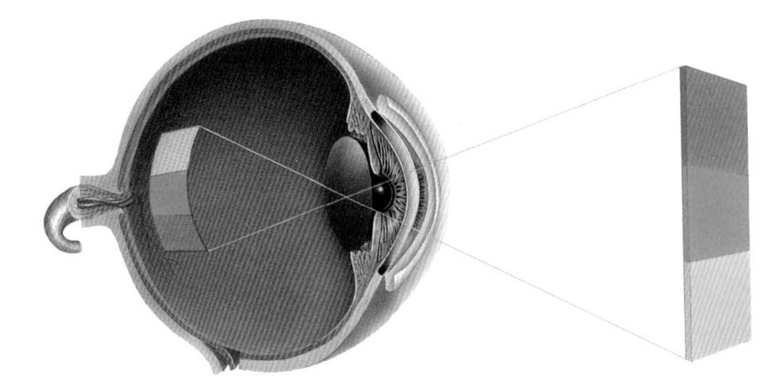

Please visit our web site at: www.garethstevens.com
For a free color catalog describing Gareth Stevens Publishing's list of high-quality books and multimedia programs, call 1-800-542-2595 or fax your request to (414) 332-3567.

Gareth Stevens Publishing would like to thank Dr. Ron Gerrits, Ph.D., Biomedical Engineering, of the Milwaukee School of Engineering, for his kind and professional help with the information in this book.

Library of Congress Cataloging-in-Publication Data

Bruno, Stephen.
The human body / by Stephen Bruno.
p. cm. — (Nature's record-breakers)
Includes bibliographical references and index.
ISBN 0-8368-2905-0 (lib. bdg.)
1. Human physiology—Juvenile literature. 2. Body, Human—Juvenile literature.
[1. Body, Human. 2. Human anatomy. 3. Human physiology.] I. Title. II. Series.
QP37.B895 2002
612—dc21 2001020534

This edition first published in 2002 by
Gareth Stevens Publishing
A World Almanac Education Group Company
330 West Olive Street, Suite 100
Milwaukee, Wisconsin 53212 USA

Translated from Italian by Christina Longman
Designer: Marco Nardi
Layout: Ornella Fassio and Adriano Nardi
Gareth Stevens editor: Monica Rausch
Gareth Stevens designer: Scott M. Krall

Printed in the United States of America

1 2 3 4 5 6 7 8 9 06 05 04 03 02

Contents

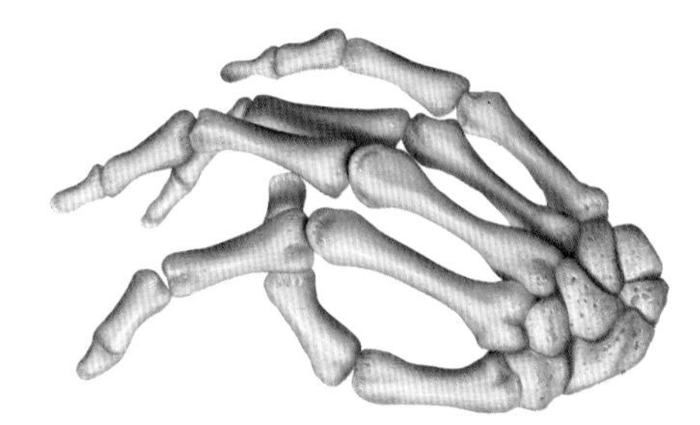

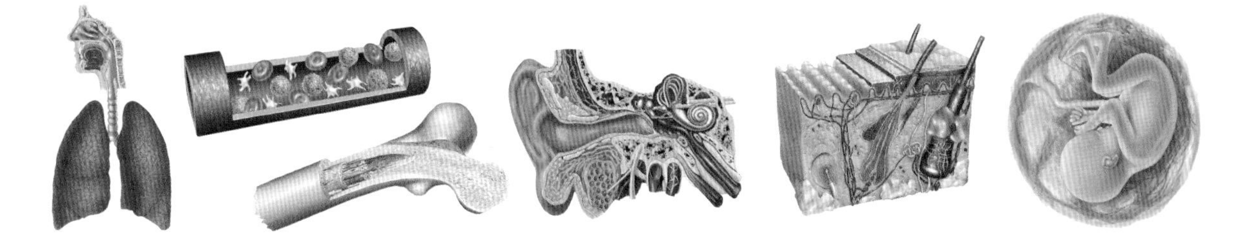

Words that appear in the glossary are printed in **boldface** type the first time they occur in the text.

The Body

The oldest **fossils** of hominids, a **species** scientists believe to be related to humans, date back approximately 5 million years. Hominids walked on two legs, just as humans do.

SPECIES	PERIOD
First hominids	5 million years ago
Australopithecus afarensis	3.5 million years ago
Australopithecus africanus	3 million years ago
Homo habilis	2.5 million years ago
Homo erectus	1.8 million years ago
Homo sapiens	120,000 years ago
Homo sapiens sapiens (humans)	100,000 years ago

Australopithecus

Homo erectus

Homo sapiens sapiens (humans)

The brain is considered to be the most important **organ** in the human body. If a person's brain stops its activity, doctors consider the person dead, even if the heart is still beating.

Venus di Milo

Men and women may look very different, but the only major differences in their anatomies are their reproductive systems.

Riace warrior

Fascinating Fact

Although people have been studying the human body for centuries, doctors and scientists began to understand the human **anatomy**, or structure of the body, better when they started studying **corpses**. Leonardo da Vinci, an Italian artist, studied corpses to create the first accurate drawings of the human anatomy. He believed this model (above) showed the proportions of a perfect body.

The human body has many different systems that work closely together. The **muscular** system, for example, sends food through the **digestive** system, while the digestive system gives **nutrients** to the muscles.

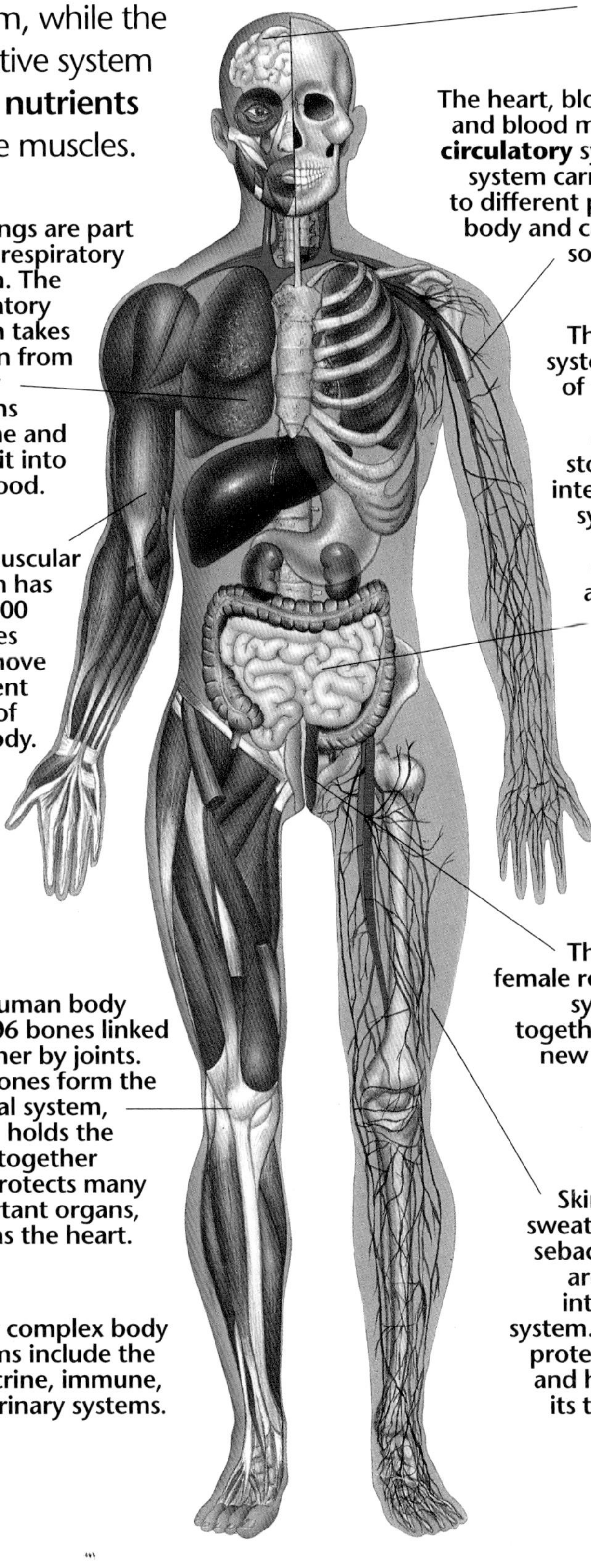

The nerves, spinal cord, and brain make up the the nervous system. This system quickly processes information from both outside and inside the body. It acts like the most complicated computer in the world!

The heart, blood vessels, and blood make up the **circulatory** system. This system carries oxygen to different parts of the body and carries away some wastes.

The lungs are part of the respiratory system. The respiratory system takes oxygen from the air humans breathe and sends it into the blood.

The digestive system consists of the mouth, teeth, esophagus, stomach, and intestines. This system turns food into energy and also gets rid of wastes.

The muscular system has over 600 muscles that move different parts of the body.

The male and female reproductive systems work together to create new human life.

The human body has 206 bones linked together by joints. The bones form the skeletal system, which holds the body together and protects many important organs, such as the heart.

Skin, hair, nails, sweat glands, and sebaceous glands are part of the integumentary system. This system protects the body and helps control its temperature.

Other complex body systems include the endocrine, immune, and urinary systems.

Did you know?

Q. What is a cell?

A. A cell is the smallest living unit in the human body that is capable of reproducing itself. Every part of the body is made of cells, and every cell specializes in a certain **function**.

Q. What is the human body made of?

A. The human body consists of over 50 trillion cells. Cells are the smallest living units in the human body. They join to make tissues, and each tissue has its own special function, or job. Tissues make up many different parts of the body, including nerves, muscles, and organs. Some organs and tissues work together to form systems. The systems act like organized "teams" to carry out a certain set of functions. The skeletal system, for example, protects the organs and supports the body as it moves. The muscular system moves different parts of the body, and the digestive system takes in nutrients the body needs to survive.

Did you know?

Q. What are neurons?

A. Neurons are the cells that make up the nervous system. These cells help the body perform basic jobs such as **regulating** all the body's functions and allowing the body to react to **stimuli**. Neurons also enable humans to think, speak, and dream.

Q. What are nerves?

A. Nerves are fibers made of very long neurons. The human body has two types of nerves: motor nerves and sensory nerves. Motor nerves make the body move by sending nervous **impulses** to the muscles. Sensory nerves react to changes in the environment, such as heat and light. The nerves turn the "sensation" of these changes into nervous signals, which they send to the brain.

Q. What parts of the body make up the nervous system?

A. The nerves, spinal cord, and brain make up the nervous system. The spinal cord and brain form the central nervous system, while a network of nerves running throughout the body forms the peripheral nervous system.

The Nervous System

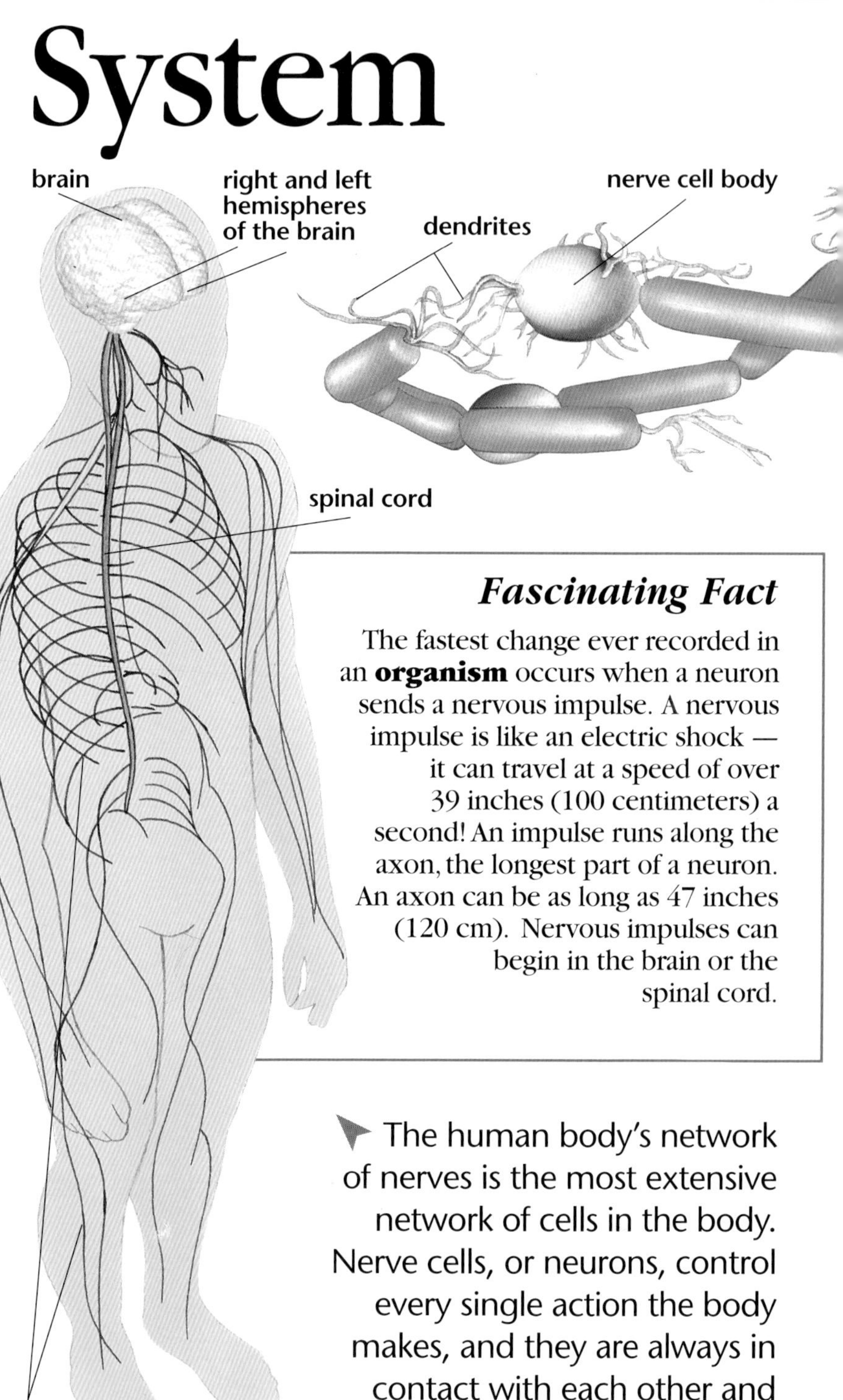

Fascinating Fact

The fastest change ever recorded in an **organism** occurs when a neuron sends a nervous impulse. A nervous impulse is like an electric shock — it can travel at a speed of over 39 inches (100 centimeters) a second! An impulse runs along the axon, the longest part of a neuron. An axon can be as long as 47 inches (120 cm). Nervous impulses can begin in the brain or the spinal cord.

The human body's network of nerves is the most extensive network of cells in the body. Nerve cells, or neurons, control every single action the body makes, and they are always in contact with each other and with other cells in the body.

axon terminals

myelin sheath that protects the nerve axon

DIAGRAM OF A NEURON (NERVE CELL)

Memory is one of the most amazing functions of the brain. Some poets in Kyrgyzstan (right), for example, have memorized the "Manas," a Kyrgyz poem over 500,000 lines long. The "Manas" is the longest poem in the world!

The human brain is the most efficient "computer" in the world. It can recognize up to 500 different tastes and distinguish up to 10,000 different colors!

The brain is the most complex organ in the human body. It is made of 15 trillion neurons and has three main parts: cerebrum, cerebellum, and brainstem. The cerebrum regulates emotions and **conscious** action; the cerebellum coordinates **involuntary** movements; and the brainstem links the brain to the spinal cord.

The cerebrum is the largest and most intelligent part of the brain. It makes up three-fourths of the brain and is responsible for conscious thoughts and emotions.

The cerebral cortex, or outer layer of the brain, has three types of areas: sensory, motor, and associative. A sensory area keeps track of sensations, such as tastes and smells. A motor area coordinates **voluntary** movements, such as walking. An associative area gathers information to form conscious thoughts.

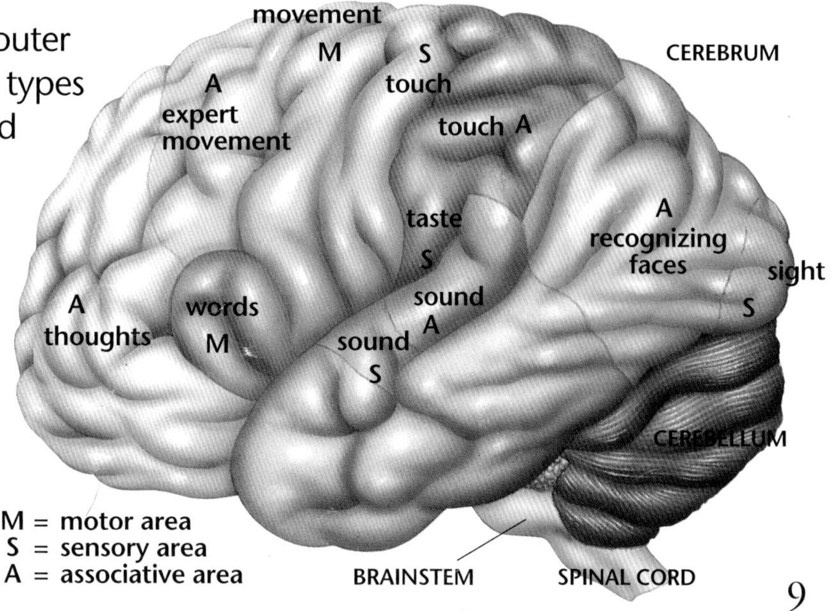

Senses

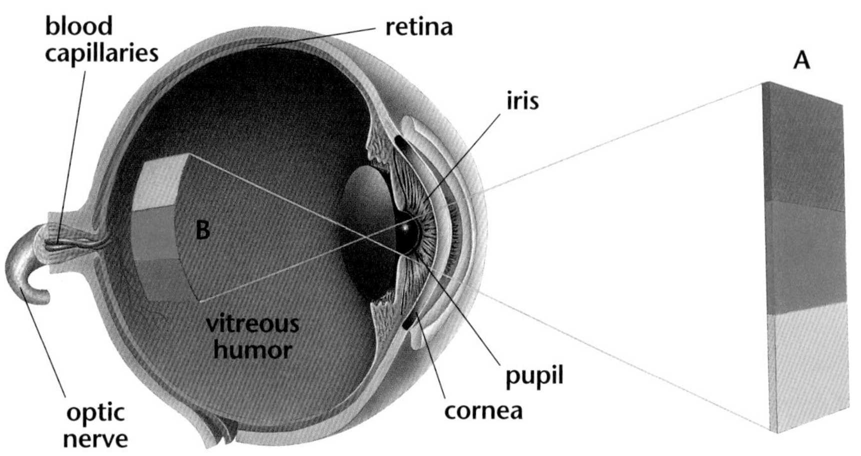

A healthy eye, in perfect condition, can distinguish almost 10,000 different shades and colors. Humans with some disorders, such as Daltonism, cannot see all of these colors.

Light reflected by an object appears upside down in the human eye. The light (A) enters the eye through the pupil, and the image is projected upside down (B) onto the retina, the back of the eye. Nerve endings in the retina send signals about the image to the brain, and the brain turns the image right-side up.

Fascinating Fact

Ludwig van Beethoven wrote wonderful music even though he was completely deaf! Rock musicians often cannot hear well, either. Constant exposure to loud noise can make a person deaf.

Nerve endings in the human ear can capture up to 1,500 different tones and up to 350 volume levels! A sound sends **vibrations** through the air. These vibrations travel through the eardrum, then through three tiny bones and into fluid in the cochlea. Nerve endings in the cochlea pick up the vibrations in the fluid.

hammer bone
stirrup bone
semicircular canal
anvil bone
auditory nerve
outer ear
outer canal
eardrum
cochlea
eustachian tube

olfactory membrane

upper jaw

soft palate

nasal cavity

teeth

jaw

esophagus

tongue

Nerve endings in the human nose can distinguish 2,000 to 4,000 different types of smells. The human mouth has over 10,000 taste buds, each of which recognizes a specific taste. The nose and mouth work closely together to sense tastes and smells.

Recognizing that food tastes bad is just as important as realizing that it tastes good. If food tastes bad, it may not be safe to eat!

Franz Xaver Messerschmidt, an Austrian artist, studied the expressions of the human face to create busts like this one (right).

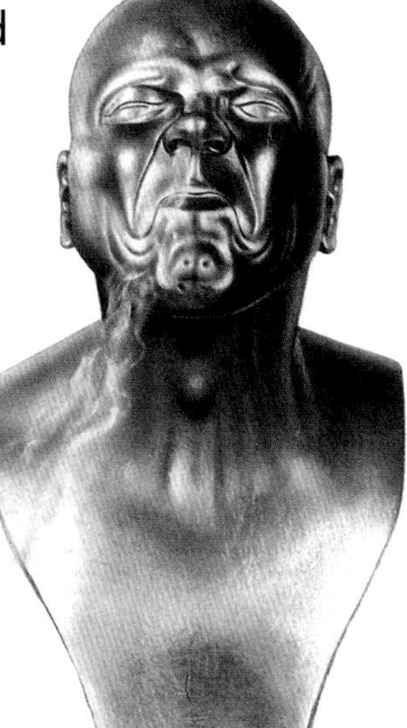

The skin is the human body's largest sense organ. Millions of nerve endings sensitive to pain, pressure, and more lie under the skin. The nerve endings in fingers help a person feel even the tiniest bumps — such as the bumps of Braille on paper.

Did you know?

Q. What is a sense organ?

A. A sense organ is an organ with lots of nerve endings. These nerve endings can pick up, or "sense," changes in the environment outside the body or changes happening inside the body. The nerve endings send information about these changes to the brain. In this way, a nervous signal can send a message about pleasant music, a beautiful landscape, a familiar face, or even a frightening sight — such as the edge of a cliff! Sensations help us to survive by keeping us out of danger.

Q. What are the main human senses?

A. The main human senses are sight, hearing, touch, taste, and smell.

Skin, Hair, and Nails

Humans have a huge variety of skin, eye, and hair colors. These colors are determined by the amount of melanin in these body parts. Melanin is a dark brown **substance** produced by certain cells in the body. People with brown hair, for example, have more melanin in their hair than people with blonde hair.

The longest human nails ever measured were 27.5 inches (70 cm) long! Nails grow from the human skin at a rate of about 2.4 inches (6 cm) a year. Nails help protect the end of the phalanx, the thin bone at the tips of fingers and toes. Human nails are made of keratin, the same substance that forms hair, and minerals that make nails hard.

Fascinating Facts

• As people grow older, their skin changes. The **elastic** tissue and muscles under skin lose their tone, and wrinkles begin to appear. Some hair follicles dry up, causing hair to fall out. Other hairs lose their color as the body gradually produces less and less melanin.

• The bodies of people with albinism cannot produce melanin. These people have milky white skin, white hair, and pale eyes.

• Hairs cover nearly every part of the body, except the soles of feet, the palms of hands, and the lips. A hair is produced by cells at the base of the hair, inside a follicle, a pit in the skin. Hairs act as sense organs. When a hair is touched, the movement from the touch is sent down the hair to nerves in the follicle. These nerves send information about the touch to the brain.

Each fingertip on a human can make a unique fingerprint that no other human has. Tiny folds in the skin of fingertips create the pattern shown in a fingerprint. Fingerprints can be used to identify people. Prints of the soles of feet and the palms of hands are also unique.

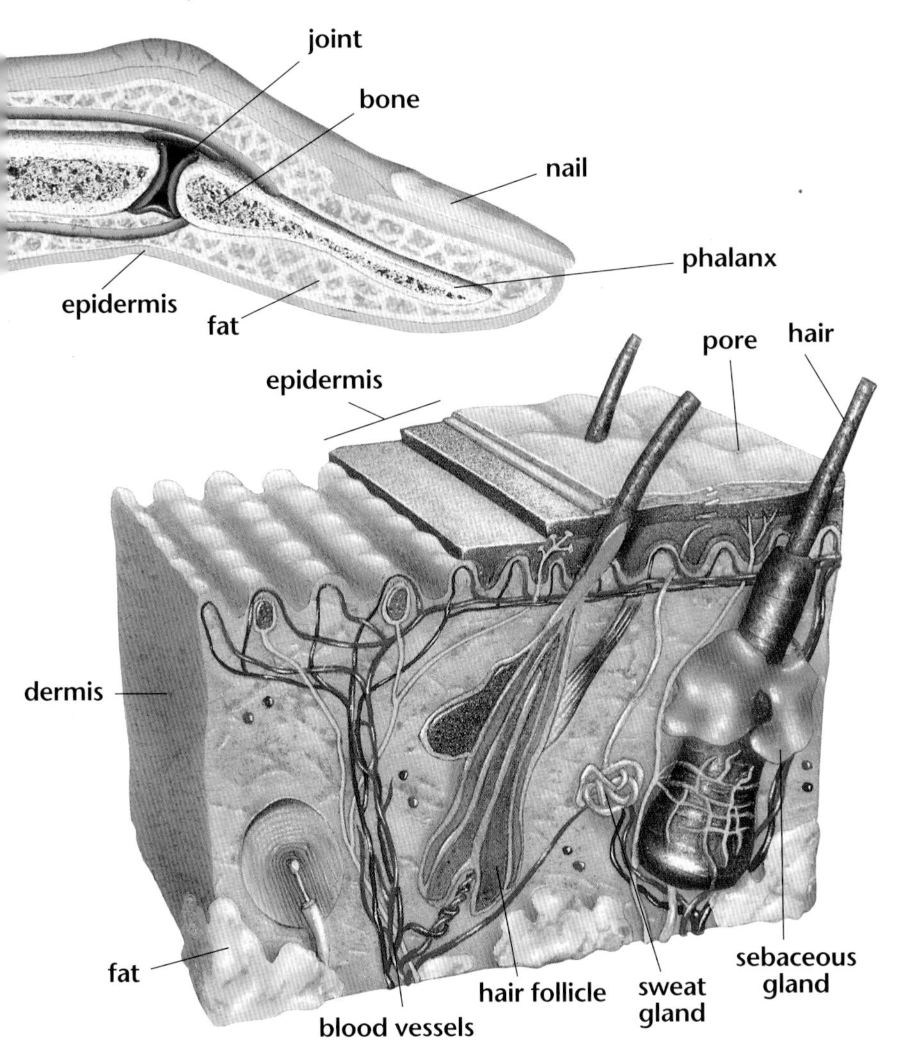

The skin is the outermost part of the human body and the largest sense organ. The uppermost layer of skin is made of dead skin cells pushed upward by the cells beneath them. This outer layer loses about 39 million dead skin cells every day! This layer of cells is part of the epidermis, the thin, outer layer of skin. Underneath the epidermis, the dermis layer of skin contains nerve endings, blood vessels, hair follicles, and sweat and sebaceous glands.

Did you know?

Q. What does skin do?

A. The skin has many functions. Skin helps sense what an object feels like — whether it is smooth or rough, solid or liquid, hot or cold. Skin also acts as a barrier and stops the body from losing too much water. Skin protects the body from the Sun's rays and helps keep the body at a constant temperature; fat under the skin insulates the body to keep it warm, and sweat from glands in the skin help cool the body. Skin is also the body's first line of defense against outside organisms. If the skin is damaged, **microorganisms** can get into the body's tissues and cause infections.

Q. What are hairs?

A. Hairs are made mainly of keratin, a hard substance that is also in fingernails and toenails. Hairs form in a follicle, a pit in the dermis layer of skin. The follicle often contains a sebaceous gland that produces oil. This oil helps keep the hair soft and flexible.

Did you **know?**

Q. What is a muscle?

A. A muscle is an organ made of muscular tissue. This tissue **contracts** or relaxes to make the body move or to make movements inside the body Muscle makes up about 40 percent of the human body.

Q. Are all muscles the same?

A. No, the human body has three main types of muscles: skeletal, smooth, and cardiac. Skeletal muscles hold bones together, move bones, and give the body shape. These muscles are the muscles that move arms and legs. Smooth muscles help different organs or tissues in the body perform certain functions. Smooth muscles around blood vessels, for example, relax and contract to push blood through the vessel. Smooth muscles around the stomach push food into the intestines. The third type of muscle, cardiac muscle, relaxes and contracts to "beat," or pump blood through, the heart.

The cutaneous muscles in the human face are the most expressive muscles in the body. A person uses 17 muscles to smile and as many as 43 muscles to frown! These muscles are similar to the muscles animals have all over their skin. A horse uses these kinds of muscles when it "shakes" its skin to get rid of flies.

The sartorius is the longest muscle in the body. It starts from the hip and stretches down as far as the outer knee. It can be over half a yard (meter) long!

gluteus maximus

The gluteus maximus, a muscle in the buttock, is one of the strongest muscles in the body. Other strong muscles include the tongue and the jaw muscles.

The skeletal muscles are the most numerous type of muscle in the human body. The body has over 600 skeletal muscles that keep the skeleton together and perform all the movements the body can make. A person uses as many as 200 muscles just to walk! Many muscles work in pairs; when one muscles contracts, the other relaxes.

Muscles

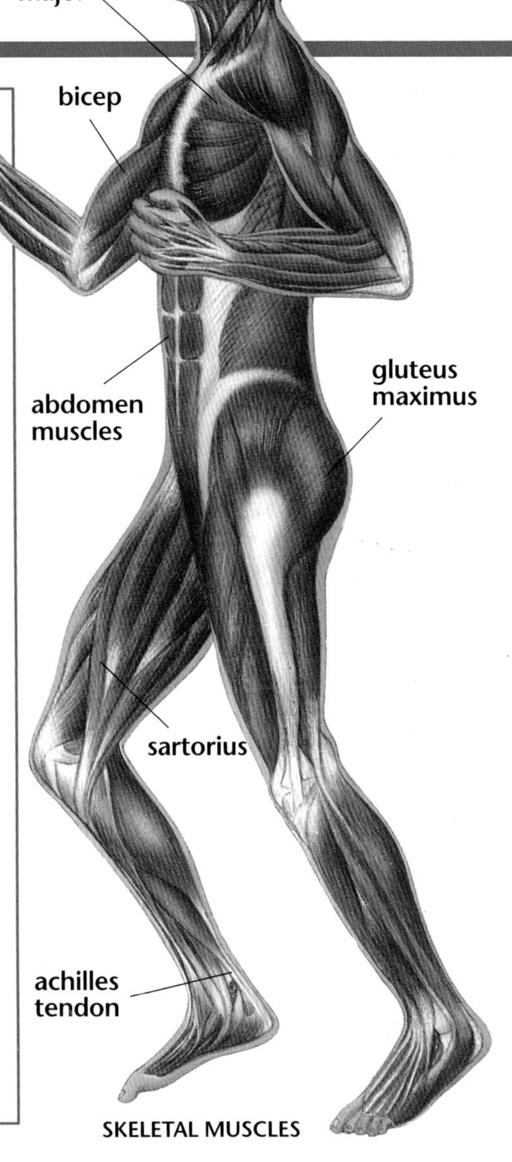

SKELETAL MUSCLES

Fascinating Facts

• The average human body produces enough energy every day to keep an electric light on for over a day and a half! The more active a body is, the more energy its muscles consume — and the more heat the body produces. Out of all the energy supplied by the nutrients and oxygen carried in the blood, however, only about 20 percent is actually used for contracting muscles.

• Skeletal muscles are usually voluntary, which means they are moved by signals sent consciously from the cerebrum. The signal to lift an arm or move a leg, for example, is voluntary. Smooth muscles are usually involuntary. They are controlled by signals sent unconsciously from the cerebellum or spinal cord. These muscles control "automatic" functions, such as passing food through the intestines or breathing.

MUSCLES OF THE HAND

The hand is the body part that can make the widest range of movements. Twenty-seven bones held together by over 30 muscles allow the hands to perform precise movements.

The Skeleton

➤ The skull has the most bones that are fused together. As many as 21 skull bones meet at joints that fuse during the first two years of life.

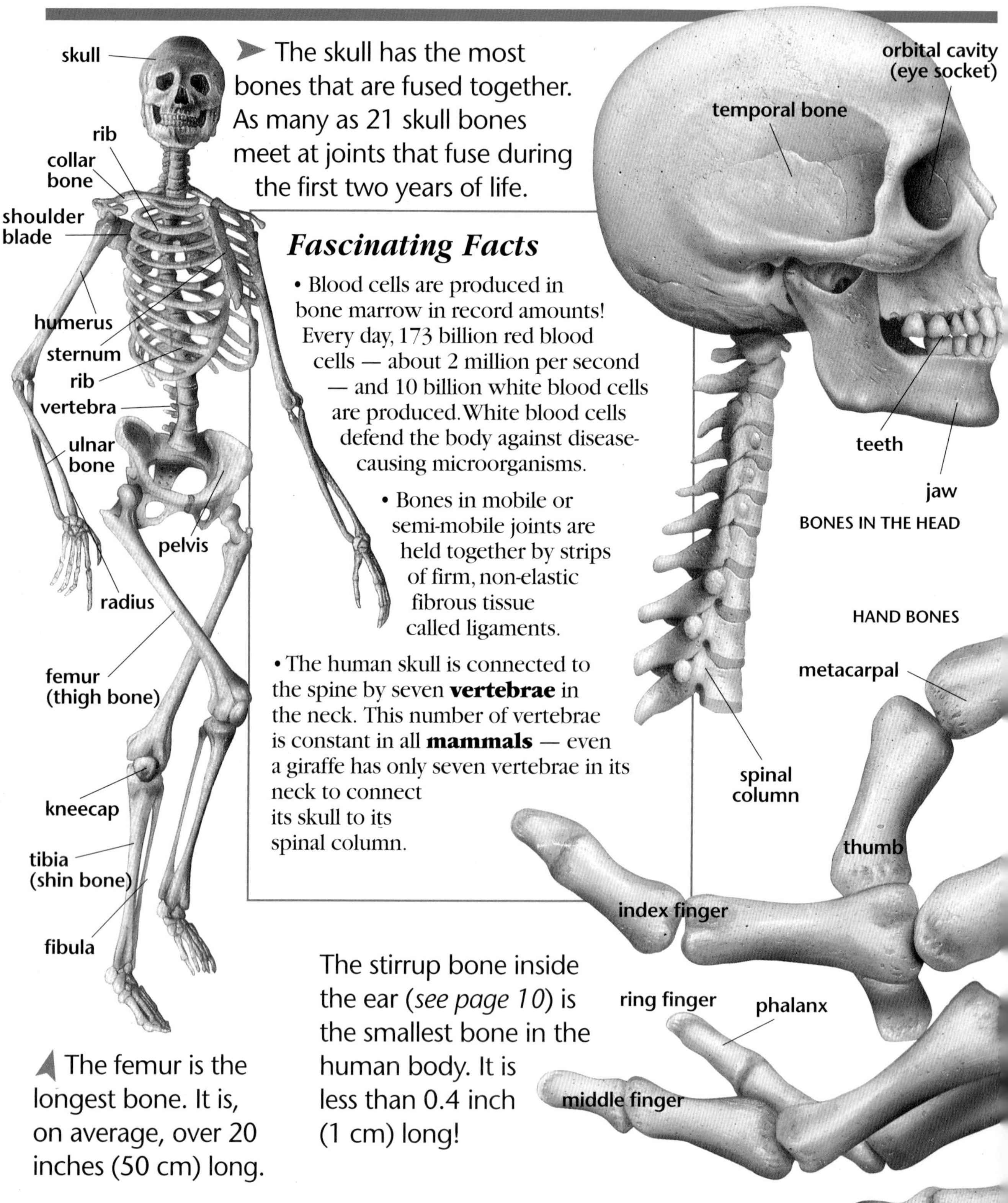

Fascinating Facts

- Blood cells are produced in bone marrow in record amounts! Every day, 173 billion red blood cells — about 2 million per second — and 10 billion white blood cells are produced. White blood cells defend the body against disease-causing microorganisms.
- Bones in mobile or semi-mobile joints are held together by strips of firm, non-elastic fibrous tissue called ligaments.
- The human skull is connected to the spine by seven **vertebrae** in the neck. This number of vertebrae is constant in all **mammals** — even a giraffe has only seven vertebrae in its neck to connect its skull to its spinal column.

The stirrup bone inside the ear (*see page 10*) is the smallest bone in the human body. It is less than 0.4 inch (1 cm) long!

◀ The femur is the longest bone. It is, on average, over 20 inches (50 cm) long.

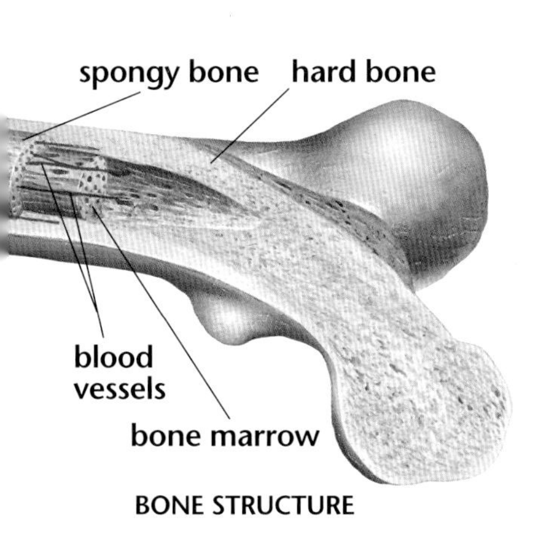

BONE STRUCTURE

The outside of a bone is made of hard lamellae. Inside, bones are made of a spongy material filled with blood vessels, nerve endings, and bone marrow, which produces blood cells and stores fat.

THE KNEE

femur

tibia

ligaments

fibula

meniscus

The knee is the largest joint in the human skeleton. The knee allows the leg to bend, and, at the same time, it supports the weight of the entire body. When bones at joints such as the knee meet, they are covered with a layer of cartilage to reduce **friction** between them.

carpal bones

knuckle bone

phalanx

The thumb joint is the only "saddle" joint in the human body. This joint allows the thumb to move forward and back as well as side to side. The thumb joint enables humans to grip objects.

Did you know?

Q. WHAT IS THE SKELETON?

A. The human skeleton is a system of bones and cartilage that protects the body's most delicate organs, holds the body together, and allows the body to move. The 206 bones in the human skeleton also contain the body's reserve of minerals, while the marrow in bones produces blood cells.

Q. WHAT IS A JOINT?

A. A joint is the part of the the skeleton where two or more bones meet. Joints can be fixed, such as the joints of skull bones; semi-mobile, such as the joints between the vertebrae in the spinal column; or mobile, such as the joints in arms and fingers.

Q. WHAT IS CARTILAGE?

A. Cartilage is a bluish-white rubbery tissue. It keeps two bones from rubbing together at joints and gives shape to a human's ears and nose. Cartilage also lines some of the airways of the respiratory system.

The Circulatory System

The human heart, on average, beats once every second — more than 100,000 times per day.

Fascinating Facts

- If we could lay all the blood vessels in a human body end to end, they would measure about 62,150 miles (100,000 km) long — over twice the distance around Earth! Every day, about 1.6 gallons (6 liters) of blood flow through this system inside an adult's human's body.
- The muscles surrounding blood vessels are involuntary; the brain does not consciously control them. Only some **hormones** can influence this muscular activity. Adrenaline, for example, can cause muscles around some blood vessels to contract.

The largest blood vessels in an adult human body can be as wide as a finger, while the smallest blood vessels, the capillaries, can be seen only under a microscope.

capillaries

carotid artery
jugular vein
aorta
heart
femoral artery
femoral vein

Blood carries oxygen from the lungs and nutrients from the intestines to other parts of the body. It also picks up carbon dioxide and other waste produced by the body. The kidneys filter out some of this waste.

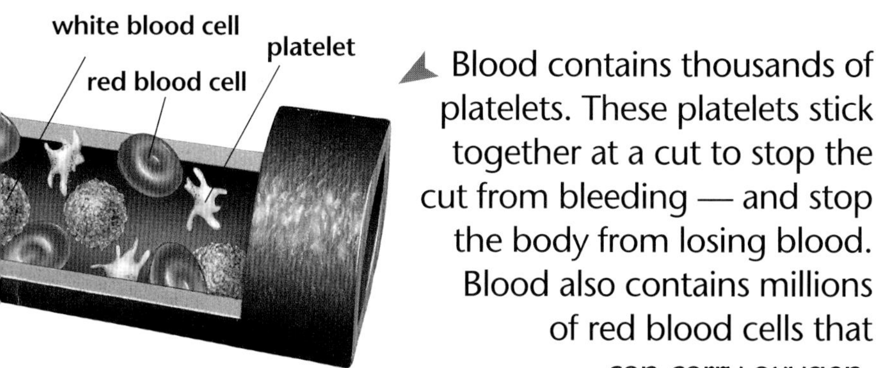

SECTION OF A BLOOD VESSEL

Blood contains thousands of platelets. These platelets stick together at a cut to stop the cut from bleeding — and stop the body from losing blood. Blood also contains millions of red blood cells that can carry oxygen.

An electrocardiogram is an instrument that can "draw" a heart beat. It helps doctors find any problems in the beating of a heart.

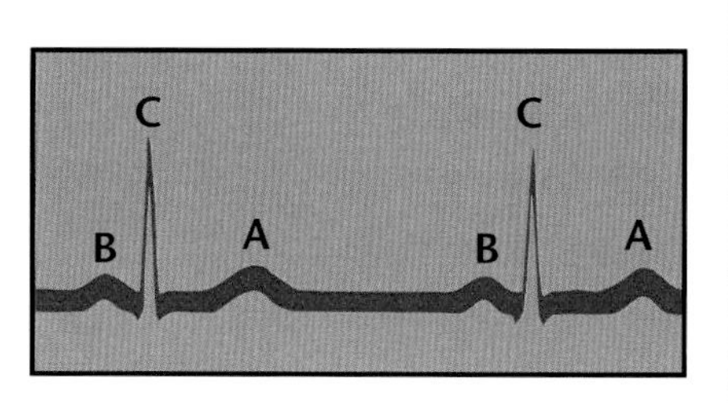

Each time the heart contracts, the electrocardiogram creates an electric pulse that jerks a pen. The pen draws this movement on a moving roll of paper. The diagram above shows the three phases of a heart beat drawn by the pen. During the first phase (A-B) the heart's atria fill with blood. During the second phase (B) the atria contract, pushing the blood into the ventricles. During the third phase (C) the ventricles contract, pumping the blood out of the heart.

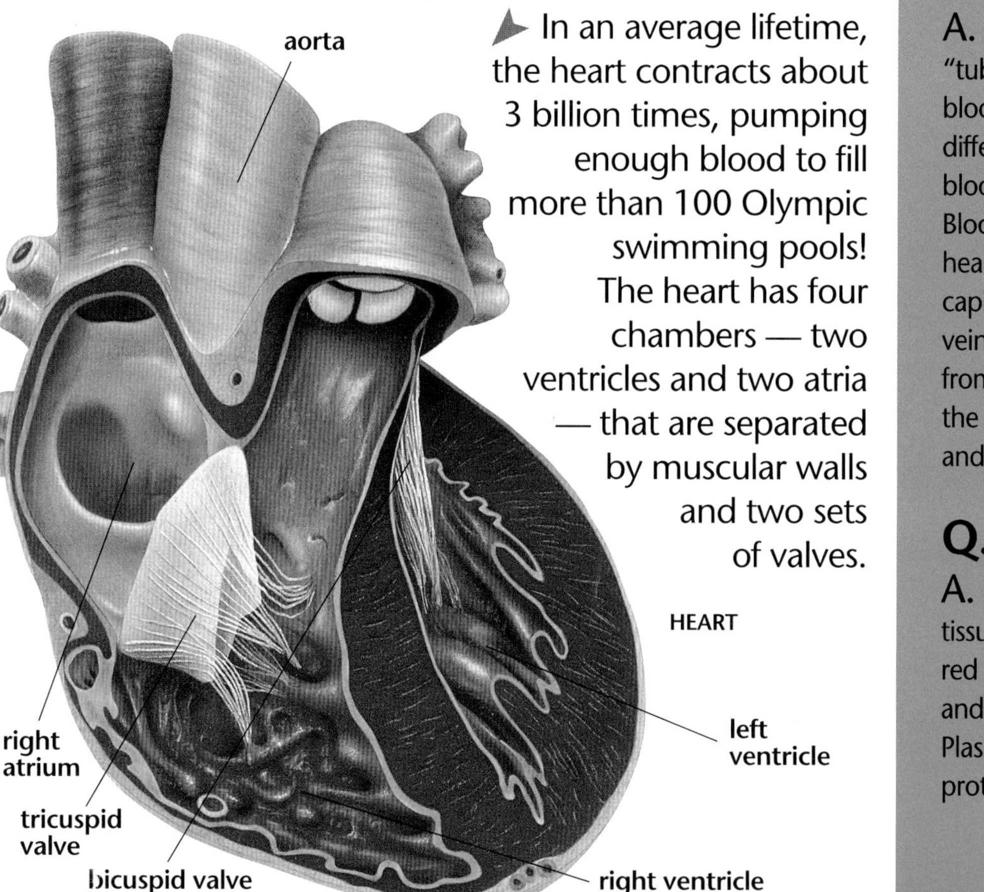

In an average lifetime, the heart contracts about 3 billion times, pumping enough blood to fill more than 100 Olympic swimming pools! The heart has four chambers — two ventricles and two atria — that are separated by muscular walls and two sets of valves.

HEART

Did you know?

Q. WHAT DOES THE CIRCULATORY SYSTEM DO?

A. The circulatory system consists of the blood vessels and the heart. It carries oxygen and nutrients to all parts of the body and carries away some waste products, such as carbon dioxide, a gas. This system also helps repair any damage done to the body, such as wounds or the loss of minerals, and protects the body from microorgansims.

Q. WHAT ARE BLOOD VESSELS?

A. Blood vessels are "tubes" through which blood flows. There are different types and sizes of blood vessels in the body. Blood flows toward the heart through the venous capillaries, venules, and veins, and it flows away from the heart through the arteries, arterioles, and arterial capillaries.

Q. WHAT IS BLOOD?

A. Blood is a half-liquid tissue made of platelets, red and white blood cells, and a liquid called plasma. Plasma is full of fats, sugars, proteins, and water.

Did you know?

Q. What is the respiratory system?

A. The respiratory system is a group of organs that take in oxygen, a gas in the air needed by cells, and **expel** water vapor and carbon dioxide. This exchange of gases is called *respiration.* Air travels through the nose; mouth; and windpipe, or trachea. The trachea splits into two bronchi, through which air enters the two lungs. Inside the lungs, the bronchi divide into smaller and smaller airways that finally end in thin-walled air sacs called alveoli.

Q. How does respiration work?

A. When a human breathes in, he or she fills 300 million alveoli with oxygen-filled air. The oxygen passes through the thin walls of the alveoli and into tiny capillaries filled with blood. The oxygen then binds with hemoglobin, a substance in red blood cells. The hemoglobin, at the same time, gets rid of the carbon dioxide it has collected from different parts of the body. The carbon dioxide passes through the wall of the alveoli and is breathed out.

The Respiratory

The air we breath out has about 100 times more carbon dioxide and half the oxygen of the air we breath in! All the cells in the body need oxygen, and they all get rid of carbon dioxide.

Air enters and leaves the body's lungs through the work of muscles that expand and contract the ribs and through the movements of the diaphragm. The diaphragm is a dome-shaped layer of muscle that separates the chest from the **abdomen**. When the diaphragm contracts, it shifts downward, creating space in the chest needed for air to fill the lungs.

Plants are important to the survival of humans. They produce the oxygen that humans breathe in, and they turn the carbon dioxide humans breathe out into nutrients. In this way, plants keep the air from containing too much carbon dioxide or too little oxygen.

System

Fascinating Fact

When humans speak or make sounds, their breathing and heart rhythms automatically change. If a person wanted to talk while keeping the same pace of breathing, the person would be out of breath and would even lose his or her balance.

epiglottis

Adam's apple

vocal cords

larynx

windpipe or trachea

esophagus

The human voice box, or larynx, is the noisiest body part! It is at the top of the windpipe and contains the vocal cords, two folds of elastic tissue. Vocal cords can make many different sounds as air passes between them.

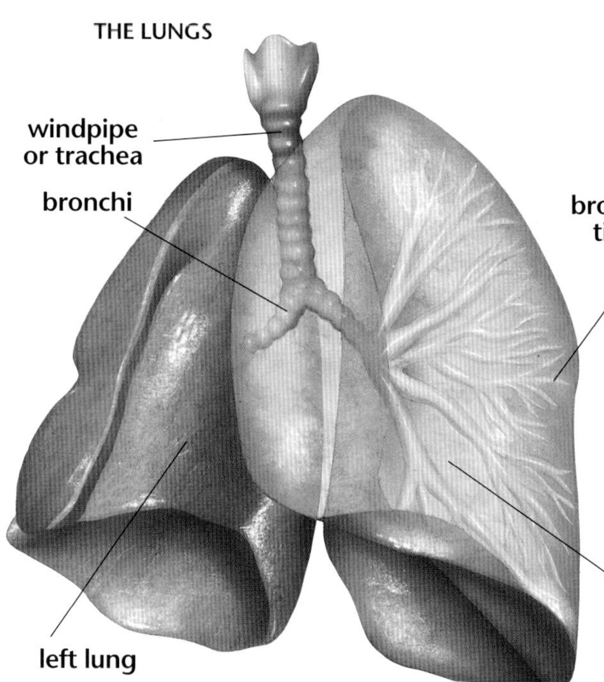

Lungs are made of an elastic tissue that can expand and contract, but this tissue is not muscular — it does not move itself. It is pulled by the movements of the diaphragm and muscles around the ribs.

Fascinating Fact

Smoking is a very unhealthy habit that affects lungs. A smoker's lung can be easily recognized at first sight. Instead of being a healthy reddish pink, the lung is grayish black. Smoking increases a person's chances of getting lung cancer.

Did you know?

Q. What does the digestive system do?

A. The digestive system processes food so that all the cells in the body can use it. The digestive system basically forms a long pathway through which the food travels. Different organs along the way produce special substances that help break down the food. The mouth produces saliva, which starts digesting sugars. The stomach **secretes** gastric juices and large amounts of pepsin, which breaks down proteins. The liver produces bile and bile salts, which turn fats into tiny droplets that are easy to digest, and the pancreas produces a juice that helps finish the digestive process. Nutrients from the food begin to enter the blood stream in the small intestines. Here, everything the body can use is **absorbed**, including water. Some undigested food and waste continue through the large intestines and are expelled from the body.

The Digestive

The mouth is the first place the digestive system begins to break down food. Teeth mash up the food, while the saliva produced here begins digesting sugars. On average, a human produces about 2,640 gallons (10,000 l) of saliva in a life time.

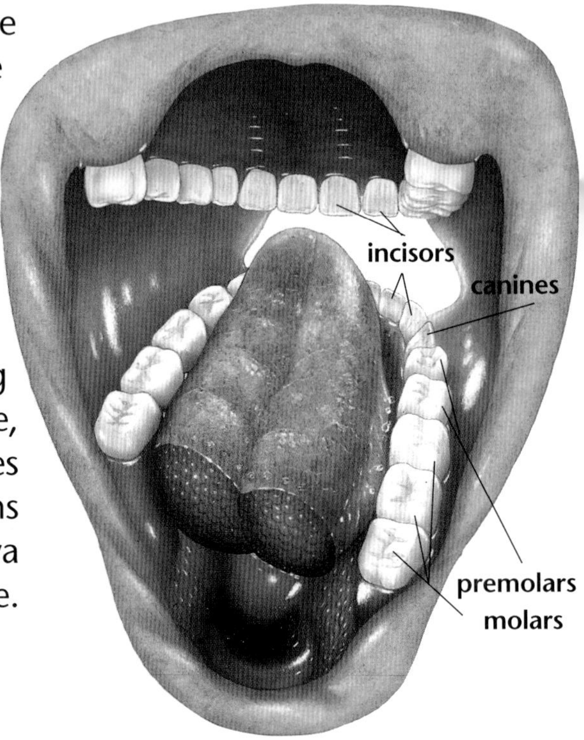

TEETH

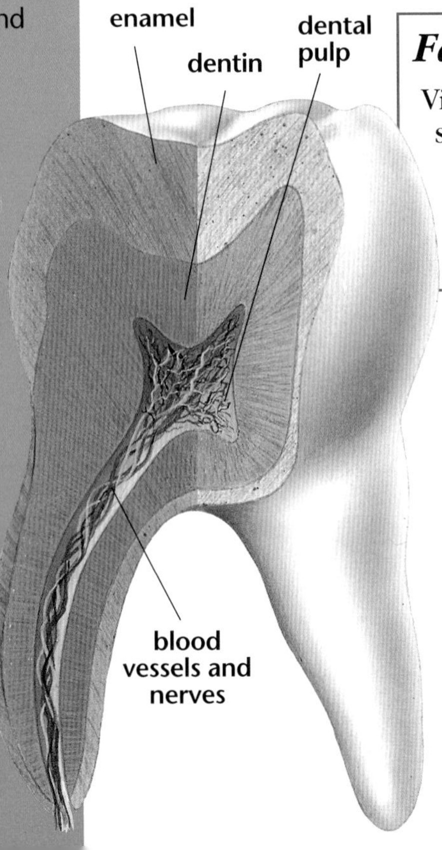

Fascinating Fact

Villi, tiny fingerlike structures inside the small intestine, help increase the area available for absorbing nutrients. The surface area of these villi is about 45 times the area covered by skin!

Teeth contain enamel, the hardest substance in the human body. Enamel completely covers the part of a tooth that appears outside the gums. Enamel is not sensitive; it is the nerve endings inside a tooth that make the tooth "feel" changes in the mouth, such as the chill of ice cream.

System

It takes about 8 seconds for food to reach the stomach after it is swallowed. The food stays in the stomach for about 2 to 6 hours, then travels to the small intestine, where it stays and is digested for about 3 to 5 hours. Unabsorbed nutrients and waste continue on to the large intestine, where they can remain from 4 hours to 3 days!

In one lifetime, about 33 tons (30 metric tonnes) of food will enter a human's stomach — the equivalent of a herd of 200 cattle!

Only the passage of food from the mouth to the esophagus is voluntary; the rest of the long digestive pathway is wrapped in involuntary muscles that push the food along without a person consciously controlling it.

esophagus
liver
stomach
small intestine
pancreas
anus
large intestine

food

The amount of energy a body can take from food is measured in calories. People who exercise or play sports need lots of energy, so they must consume more calories a day. Calories the body does not need are stored as fat. Too much fat in the body can cause health problems, so doctors recommend taking in only the amount of calories a person's body needs.

AVERAGE ENERGY REQUIREMENTS IN CALORIES PER DAY	
newborn baby up to 1 year	850
woman who is not very active	1,900
child (8 years old)	2,000
active woman	2,150
girl (15 years old)	2,200
man who is not very active	2,500
breast-feeding woman	2,685
boy (15 years old)	3,000
active man	3,000

Did you know?

Q. What is reproduction?

A. Reproduction is the process by which two organisms create a new organism.

Q. How do humans reproduce?

A. A male sperm cell makes contact with a female egg cell. The two cells fuse, or merge together, to form a single cell, called a zygote. The zygote contains all the information needed to build a new human body. It begins reproducing itself by dividing in half. The two halves produce new halves, then each of these new cells divides. In this way, the zygote develops into a morula, a ball of cells that are all the same type. The morula settles inside the uterus of the mother and receives all its nutrients from the mother. In the next nine months, the morula grows and develops into a human baby.

Reproduction

sperm cells

egg

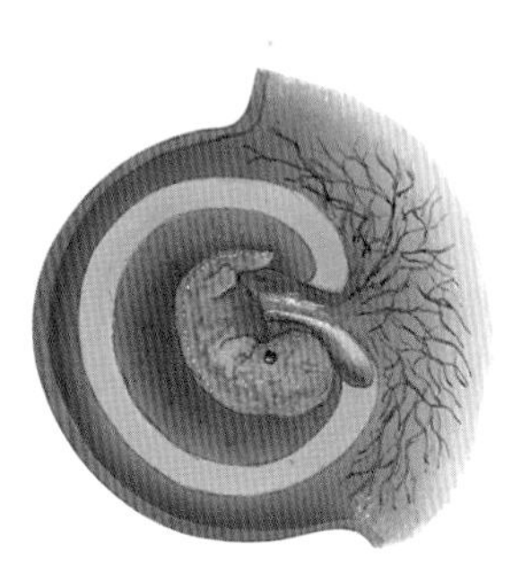

4 WEEKS

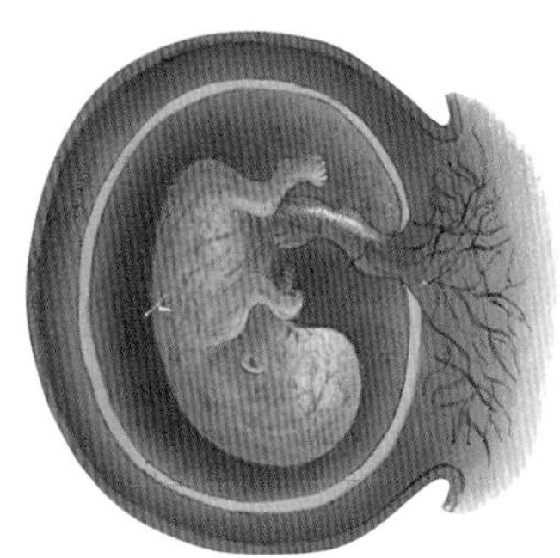

6 WEEKS

A single cell, called a zygote, grows into an organism with billions of cells in just nine months. During this time, about 200 bones develop, as do hundreds of muscles, tens of special organs, and a brain about one-fourth the size of an adult's.

4 MONTHS

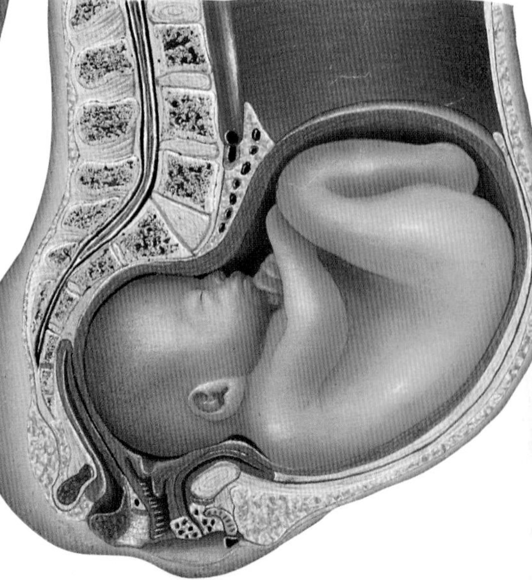

9 MONTHS

and Growth

A woman usually releases only one egg at a time, while a man produces millions of spermatozoa, or sperm cells. An egg cell fuses with only one of these spermatozoa to form a zygote.

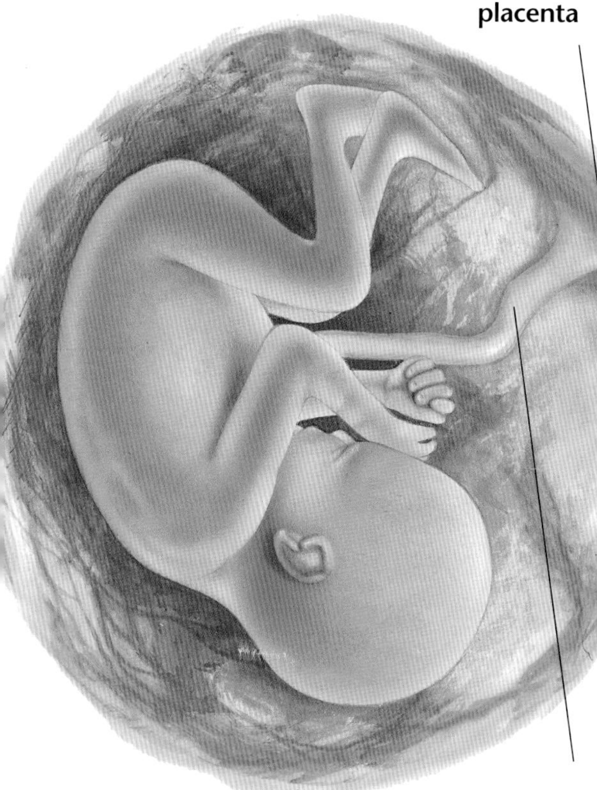

A fetus has all the parts of a human body, although some of these parts are not yet working. A fetus, for example, still gets food from its mother through the placenta, a tissue that allows minerals, water, and nutrients to pass from the mother to the baby.

Fascinating Fact

Humans begin to "age" when more cells in the body die than are replaced. In fact, when a baby is born, it doesn't age. Instead, it continues to grow until it reaches maturity, the moment it is fully developed. Different organs in a human reach maturity at different times. Bones, for example, stop growing after about 18 years, but their cells still reproduce to replace the cells that die. The brain, on the other hand, stops growing at 15 years; after that, about 100,000 neurons die every day, without being replaced.

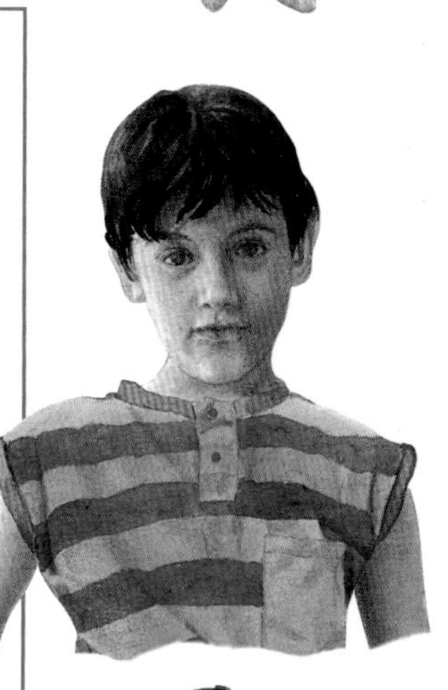

Cells, Genes,

STRUCTURE OF A CELL

nucleus

cytoplasm

plasma membrane

mitocondrion

ribosome

golgi body

The cell is the smallest part of the human body. Although cells perform different functions, all cells have the same basic structure. Each part of a cell carries out a special function in the cell. The nucleus acts like the cell's "brain." The mitochondria turn nutrients into energy, while ribosomes build material needed for the cell to reproduce.

Identical twins are the only humans who share the exact same genes. Identical twins are produced by the same zygote, which split into two cells that developed into two separate babies.

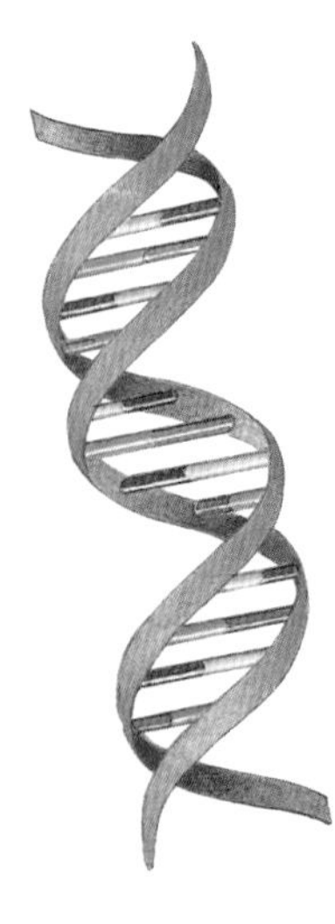

DNA

Did you know?

Q. What is DNA?

A. DNA is short for deoxyribonucleic acid. Chromosomes are made of this substance and proteins.

Q. What is a gene?

A. A gene is a tiny unit of DNA in a chromosome. Genes determine what qualities the entire organism, or person, will have. A gene, for example, can determine hair color or eye color. Genes are **hereditary**, which means that they are passed from parents to children.

Q. What are chromosomes?

A. Chromosomes are a chain of genes. Each animal species has a certain number of chromosomes in its cells. Humans typically have 46 chromosomes in the nucleus of almost every cell in their bodies. Egg and sperm cells contain just half that number, so when a sperm and egg join, the new zygote will have a full set of chromosomes. The zygote then gets half its genes from the mother, through the egg, and half from the father, in the sperm.

and Hormones

The endocrine system is made up of glands that produce hormones. Each gland produces a different hormone that performs a specific function. The pancreas, for example, produces insulin, a hormone that regulates the amount of sugar in the blood.

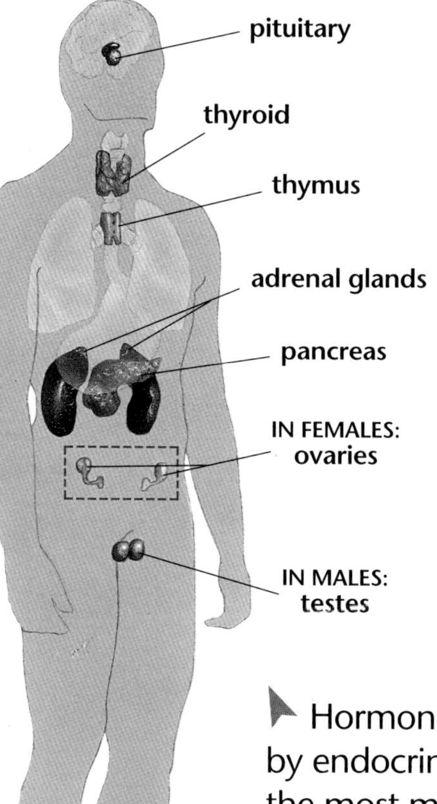

Fascinating Fact

If no new babies were born, in just a few decades, no more humans would be alive on Earth. In some countries, however, the number of babies born every year is much larger than the number of people dying, so the population is growing. To stop this growth, some countries limit the number of babies one person can have.

Hormones produced by endocrine glands are the most mysterious substances in the body — doctors are still identifying all the functions they perform.

Fascinating Fact

Every day the human body produces billions of new cells. These new cells are produced when old cells divide in half. Each half of an old cell grows a new half, to make two completely new cells. The genes in the nucleus of the old cell also split in half and form two new halves, so each new cell has a full set of genes.

The most noticeable qualities a human receives from parents are hair and eye colors. They are hereditary characteristics.

Going for Greatness

Humans can learn new languages and physical functions best in early childhood, when the brain is still growing. Older children, however, are better at learning abstract ideas, such as ideas in math and science.

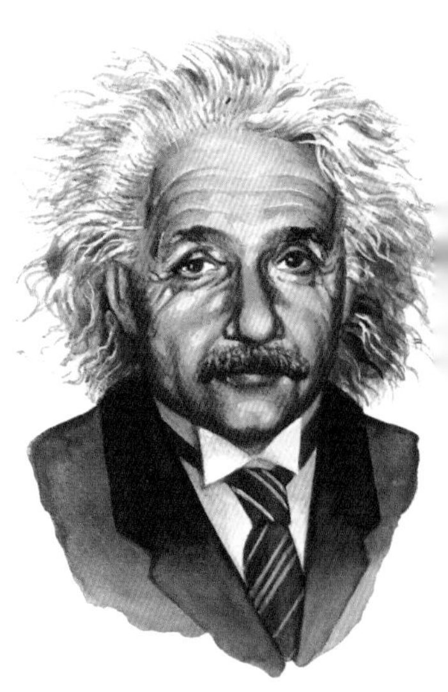

Albert Einstein

Some people believe a human must balance the needs of the body and the mind to be completely healthy and "whole." Some martial arts, for example, work not only to train the body, but also to develop and focus the mind.

Pablo Picasso

Humans have used their minds to produce great works in science, literature, art, and more. Albert Einstein, for example, made many scientific discoveries that led to the development of nuclear energy. Artist Pablo Picasso created many memorable paintings.

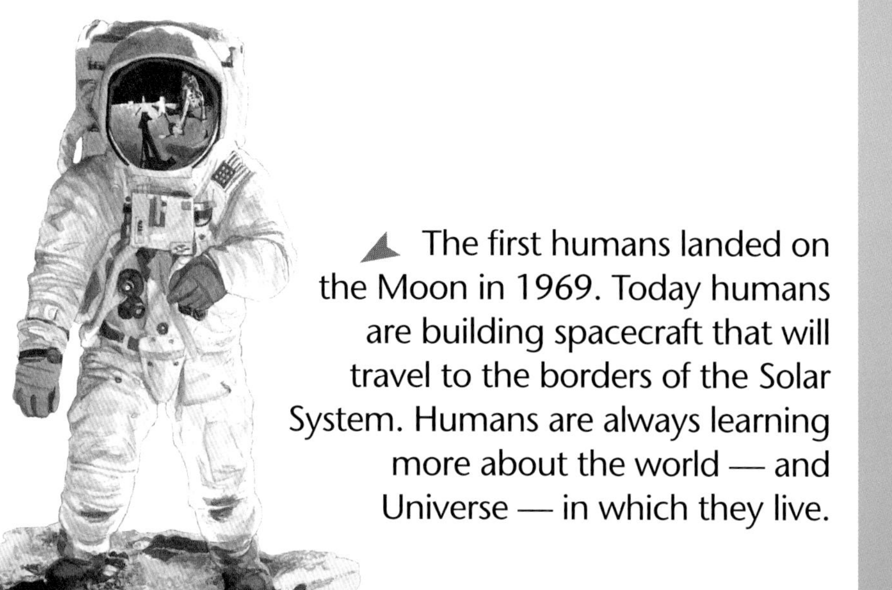

The first humans landed on the Moon in 1969. Today humans are building spacecraft that will travel to the borders of the Solar System. Humans are always learning more about the world — and Universe — in which they live.

World Record-holders in Track and Field

	MEN		WOMEN	
100 m	9.79"	Maurice Greene (U.S.)	10.49"	Florence Griffith-Joyner (U.S.)
200 m	19.32"	Michael Johnson (U.S.)	21.34"	Florence Griffith-Joyner (U.S.)
400 m	43.18"	Michael Johnson (U.S.)	47.60"	Marita Koch (Germany)
800 m	1' 41.11"	Wilson Kipketer (Denmark)	1' 53.28"	Jamila Kratochvilova (Czech Republic)
5,000 m	12' 39.36"	Haile Gebrselassie (Ethiopia)	14' 28.09"	Jiang Bo (China)
10,000 m	26' 22.75"	Haile Gebrselassie (Ethiopia)	29' 31.78"	Wang Junxia (China)
High Jump	2.45 m	Javier Sotomayor (Cuba)	2.09 m	Stefka Kostadinova (Bulgaria)
Pole Vault	6.14 m	Sergey Bubka (Ukraine)	4.63 m	Stacy Dragila (U.S.)
Long Jump	8.95 m	Mike Powell (U.S.)	7.52 m	Galina Chistyakova (Soviet Union)
Shot Put	23.12 m	Randy Barnes (U.S.)	22.63 m	Natalya Lisovskaya (Soviet Union)
Discus	74.08 m	Jürgen Schult (Germany)	76.80 m	Gabriele Reinsch (Germany)
Hammer	86.74 m	Yuriy Sedykh (Soviet Union)	76.07 m	Michaela Melinte (Romania)
Javelin	98.48 m	Jan Zelezny (Czech Republic)	69.48 m	Trine Solberg-Hattestad (Norway)

Humans can perform amazing physical feats. World record-holders in short distance running have reached speeds of 23 miles (37 km) per hour!

Did you know?

Q. How does a person become a great athlete, scientist, artist, or musician?

A. What a person does or becomes in his or her lifetime depends both on the genes the person **inherits** and on the environment in which the person lives. A son or daughter of a musician, for example, may have inherited the ability to appreciate or create great music, but if that son or daughter is not encouraged by parents or by other people to develop or improve the ability, then he or she most likely will not become a musician. Becoming a great musician, artist, scientist, or thinker takes a lot of time, patience, and determination.

Glossary

abdomen: the part of the body containing the stomach and intestines; belly.

absorbed: taken in; soaked up.

anatomy: the structure of the human body.

circulatory: relating to circulation, the process by which blood flows through the body.

conscious: aware of one's surroundings; able to feel and think; awake.

contracts: squeezes together; tightens.

corpses: dead bodies of humans.

digestive: relating to digestion, the process in which the body breaks down food and takes nutrients from it.

elastic: bendable; flexible.

expel: get rid of.

fossils: traces or remains of animals or plants from an earlier period of time.

friction: the rubbing of one object against another.

function: duty; job; task.

hereditary: received from one's parents.

hormones: substances produced by a gland or organ in the body to control certain processes, such as growth.

impulses: messages sent from one neuron to another in the human body.

inherits: receives qualities or characteristics from one's parents.

involuntary: in the human body, relating to a movement made without conscious thought. Instead, the movement is made as a result of messages sent unconsciously from the spinal cord or cerebellum.

mammals: warm-blooded animals that feed their babies on milk and usually give birth to live young.

microorgansims: tiny living things that often can only be seen with the help of a microscope.

muscular: made of muscle tissue, a tissue that can be tightened or stretched.

nutrients: proteins, minerals, and other matter the body needs to survive and grow.

organ: a part of a human or animal that is made of different tissues organized to perform a certain function.

organisms: living things.

regulating: controlling and keeping a process at a certain speed or a substance at a certain level. Insulin, for example, regulates the amount of sugar in the blood.

secretes: produces and releases a substance inside the body.

species: animals or plants that are closely related. Members of the same species can breed together.

stimuli: something that produces a response in the body, making it react a certain way.

substance: the basic material out of which something is made.

vertebrae: bones in the spinal column, or backbone, of a human.

vibrations: rapid movements up and down or back and forth.

voluntary: in the human body, relating to a movement made through conscious thought. Arm movements, for example, are voluntary movements.

More Books to Read

101 Things Every Kid Should Know about the Human Body. Samantha Beres (NTC Publishing)

The Bones and Skeleton Game Book. Karen C. Anderson and Stephen Cumbaa (Workman Publishing Company)

Guide to the Human Body: A Photographic Journey through the Human Body. Richard Walker (DK Publishing)

Inside the Human Body. An Inside Look (series). Kate Barnes (Gareth Stevens)

The Living World. Record Breakers (series). David Lambert (Gareth Stevens)

Medicine. History News (series). Phil Gates (Gareth Stevens)

The Science of the Human Body. Living Science (series). Lauri Seidlitz (Gareth Stevens)

Why Don't Haircuts Hurt? Questions and Answers about the Human Body. Melvin and Gilda Berger (Scholastic)

Yikes! Your Body Up Close. Mike Janulewicz (Simon and Schuster Trade)

Videos

A Healthy Body. Tell Me Why (series). (Vision Quest Video)

Human Body for Children Video Series. (Schlessinger)

Human Body: The Inside Scoop. Bill Nye the Science Guy (series). (Disney)

Secrets of the Code. 3 2 1 Contact (series). (PBS Home Video)

Web Sites

Yucky Gross and Cool Body
yucky.kids.discovery.com/noflash/body/index.html/

DNA: An Introduction
www.eurekascience.com/ICanDoThat/dna_intro.htm

BBC Online: Science: The Human Body
www.bbc.co.uk/science/humanbody/standard/index.shtml

Hillendale Health: Learn about the Body
hes.ucf.k12.pa.us/gclaypo/health_index.html

Some web sites stay current longer than others. For further web sites, use a search engine, such as www.yahooligans.com, to locate the following keywords: *brain, cells, circulation, digestion, ear, eyes, genes, heart, hormones, human body, muscles, senses, skeleton,* and *skin.*

Index